The Last Ride

The Last Ride

A REAL LIFE STORY OF LOVE, HOPE & DETERMINATION WHICH OVERPOWER DESTINY

Dr. Ashok Sharma

PARTRIDGE

To order additional copies of this book, contact
Partridge India
000 800 10062 62
orders.india@partridgepublishing.com

www.partridgepublishing.com/india

CONTENTS

To the memory of my
beloved daughter
Sugandh

ABOUT THE AUTHOR

Author, Dr. Ashok Sharma was born in Ajmer City and studied medicine there. He is serving as Physician in Delhi and National Capital Region for the last 25 years. He wrote health related tips in various local newspapers and magzines. He is also an associate member of Western India Film writer association and also the member of Western India Film producers association. He also produced two short documentary films "Firdoosi" and "The Silent Killer – Diabetes".

PREFATORY

ISHI VASISHTA, A very holy sage from india, in his discourse to Lord Rama in the famous "YOG VASISHTA" observed linking of soul and body is birth, continued linkage is life, delinking is death and relinking is rebirth. Known by all, birth and death are unending cycles in the universe for millions of years. Every birth creates vibrations mentally and physically and they are beyond imagination and emotions, so is death.

BHAGWAT GITA the celestial song revered all over the world says "one who is born has to die and one who dies has to be reborn. (JATASYA HE DHRUVAM MRTUTUH DRUVAM JANMA MRUTASYA CHA)

All over the world, Para-Psychologists were doing research on the various theories propounded on 'LIFE AFTER DEATH'. Ian Stevenson a century ago and sudip bhattacharya did a lot of formulations, supported by case studies, to prove that rebirth is possible in a variety of manifestations. In the west, many centuries old philosophers like pythogorous, Socrates and plato, expressed their firm belief in reincarnation of souls.

Hindu beliefs were in firm existence since many centuries earlier. Neoplatoneism, Orphism, Hermeticism and Manicheanism and Gnosticism of roman era, championed such belief in rebirth after death.

Bhavishyat Purna, a fascinating Indian treatise on 'Life after Death' profoundly dwells on several phases on transmigration of souls and their manifestation in humans, animals, birds and fish and under-water living creatures. (BHU CHARA, KHE CHARA AND JALA CHARA)

Here is a short book containing a narration of what has happened in the first part of the 21st century in a mystic and unbelievable form. Dr.

Ashok Sharma, an element practicing and god-fearing doctor wedded to another Dr. Uma Sharma in Delhi, is a happy family enjoying treating patients, particularly poor patients of all kinds free and feeling happy when they recover, from their diseases and reach their homes.

They had a happy family consisting of a grown up daughter known as 'Sugandh' and a son by name 'Prabhat'. They were a happy go lucky family enjoying life to the fullest extent. Dr. Ashok Sharma and his wife Dr. Uma Sharma are busy medical practitioners loved passionately by their patients, for their devotion, competency and dedication for looking after their well being.

In life happiness and unhappiness, pleasure and pain, good times and badtime come many times suddenly without any linking of their seriousness. In this family of happy souls wishing welfare of suffering many, One day a thunderbolt dropped from the blue shattering the ocean of happiness they have been enjoying. 'Sugandh' the grown up daughter of the devoted doctor – couple, developed serious respiratory problems. Both the doctors, who achieved a level of eminence in their fields, tried their utmost to save her, yet fate choose to take her soul away from them, drowning the whole family in a ocean of sorrow.

All souls in the family felt shocked and suffered imbalance in every field in the following days, months and years. Here comes the new phase of unknown soul technology. In east as well as west, souls after death, some times detach from the known souls, some time refuse to leave the living souls, come what may. "Sugandh" soul appears to have decided to be firmly undetachable from the father, mother and younger brother, leave alone grand parents. Her death shocked beyond words, every soul in the family and a yearning started and she must come back. And they felt they cannot live without her.

In the following months she came in dreams of her friends and told them she is coming. Different times her father, mother and brother were also told in their dreams by her that she would be coming too soon than they ever hoped. When they mentioned to their relatives and friends what she told them no one believe it and thought they were having hallucinations and are mentally disturbed.

Hope is basis of life. A soul coming back to own mother is unheard of in the known history of parapsycohology. Dr. Uma Sharma, aged 46, mother of the departed daughter, Sugandh became suddenly pregnant, usually not possible for anyone to believe, in view of her age. As per bhavishya purana, a soul after death splits usually up to five sub-soul, called panch prana. Undergoing through difficult and very risky delivery, she gave birth to twins male children. One had a long hair like a girl and the other crisp. Flood of happiness returned to the family in abundance thereafter.

This is the long and short of the narrative, in form of a book, of return of the lost dear soul split into two, filling two bodies. Both the twins are excellent and occupying the same room in which 'Sugandh' lived in her times.

I wish and all success and peace to the family. This novel experience in para-psychology is expressed in literary mould by the author.

DR. GVG KRISHNAMURTY

Former Election Commissioner of India

Place: New Delhi

Date: 18.05.2016

ACKNOWLEDGEMENT

I owe a deep sense of gratitude to all my patients who pray for the well being of my family.

I sincerely thank Mr. N. P. Singh a well known producer at film industry, Mumbai for constant encouragement and inspiration in my literary pursuit.

I am extremely thanks to Partridge India, A Penguin Random House Company, Bloomington for publishing this book is excellent manner.

Special thanks are due to my son Prabhat Sharma for designing the front cover and back page of this book.

I would like to place on record the contribution of my family friends Mr. D.K. Pandey and Mr.

G.V. Rao for their invaluable suggestions during the writing of this book.

I am highly indebted to my wife Dr. Uma Sharma for her unstinted support and corporation in my literary pursuit.

In addition, I wish to acknowledge with deep sense of gratitude to Dr. P. Kumar, Mr. Avasthi, Ms. Manisha Joshi, Mr. Sumit Sharma and Mr. Deepak Gautam for helping in editing the book.

FOREWORD

Twenty years ago, I also came to this metro as a Resident Doctor. I wanted to live in Delhi, and gain some experience. I was born in a small town, Ajmer. I finished all of my studies, from birth till my M.D., within a small radius of 3 kilometers. It had just been three months since I was married. My wife Uma was also a Junior Demonstrator in the pathology department of Medical College in Rohtak, which was located 70 kilometers away from Delhi. In fact, she appeared for an interview for this very post at 3 PM on our wedding day. She had skillfully managed to hide her completely henna-colored hands in her white doctor's coat.

Time flies in metro cities, and when you have to perform ICU duty, you just cannot keep track of day and night. Even after finishing a 24-hour duty, I never took a break. After leaving the hospital, I would take a bus straight to Rohtak and come back next morning at 7 for my next shift. Whenever I got a couple of days off, I would go to Ajmer. Thus, passed a year…dealing with jostling and pushing in public buses.

In the meantime, Uma left her job in Rohtak and joined here as a Resident Doctor in Delhi. She gave birth to our beautiful daughter Sugandh. By now, I had become totally attuned to the hectic life of this metro city. I had already spent 3 years in Delhi. Uma gave birth to Prabhat. I had my own clinic now, and I was a really busy man. From 7 in the morning till 11 at night, I would work as a consultant in the neighboring hospitals and see patients in my clinic and at home as well. Later on, I bought my own apartment and opened a lab in my clinic for Uma.

Ten years had passed since we came to Delhi. We had set up our own nursing home and within just 12 years of moving to Delhi, we became owners of a spacious bungalow. We attributed our incredible success to the grace of Almighty. We staunchly believed that Goddess Lakshmi and Goddess Saraswati, both were very kind to us and we worked day and night, driven by the fear of offending God. Uma was a religious woman and hence, religious events like *kathas* and *kirtans* were a part of daily routine in our home. We had led a very austere life so far. It was a different matter, however, that in order to achieve so much in so little time, we had to become totally oblivious to our respective families. Forget about attending weddings in the family, I couldn't even manage to visit them when my aunt and uncle passed away. I had forgotten everything and everyone for the sake of my patients.

By now, Sugandh had finished her schooling and was attending university. Prabhat was in the ninth grade. I hadbegun to feel that I was very close to fulfilling my life goals. So, I should cut down on work.

My parents and Uma, both were concerned about my health. They would say, "You are getting old, you should not exhaust yourself so much."

I would reply with a smile, "I would keep working as long as I have enough stamina by the grace of God. And in any case, it is just a matter of a few years. Let Sugandh get married and Prabhat leave for abroad; I will cut down on my work to nearly half of what I do now." I don't know how God got wind of what I said, and he didn't like it at all. And so, overnight, he turned my life upside down.

PART I

t was the night of 18th April. Yes, I remember it very well. It was 10.30 P.M. Following my daily routine, I was attending to the last lot of patients in my clinic. The sound of TV was reverberating in the lobby, and it helped me guess that not more than one or two patients were in the waiting. And then, it was Saturday. I always used to be in a hurry to reach home on Saturdays. My 14-year old son Prabhat and 18-year old daughter would keep calling up *Bhaiyya* at the reception desk and asking how long daddy would take to reach home. It was only on Saturday nights that they were allowed to stay up late with their daddy. Rest of the days, their mummy Dr. Uma would send them to bed before their daddy reached home. *What if they don't get up on time the next day and get late for school?* The moment the last OPD patient entered the chamber, my mobile started ringing. Someone was calling from abroad. So, I picked it up immediately. My friend Arun was on the line. I knew that he was a doctor in Oman. I said, "Arun! When did you arrive in Delhi? It has been over a year since you called me up." Before I could finish my queries, he interrupted me and said in a very troubled voice, "Save all that for later. Ashok, listen carefully, my son Aniruddh is an interior designer,and he lives in Hauz Khas, and he is having an asthma attack at the moment. I am in Oman and cannot help him at all. Please do something, my friend!" I replied quickly, "Hauz Khas is 20 kilometers away from my place. It is 11 P.M. now. And considering the condition he is in at the moment, he cannot travel to my clinic. So, please pass on my mobile number to him immediately,and I will tell him about the medicine or get him admitted to a nearby hospital." Saying that I disconnected the call and hurriedly got busy with the patient sitting in front of me. Suddenly, the phone rang again. I was nearly sure that it was Aniruddh's call, and so I picked up the receiver and said, "Yes, dear! Arun has explained everything to me. Here are the names of a syrup and two tablets. Write them down and ask someone to get them immediately from the medical store. If you do not get any relief, do call me again after an hour."

It was already past 11.30 P.M. when I left my clinic and sat in the car to leave for home. I began to prepare myself mentally to face my daughter Sugandh's displeasure. The moment I blew the horn in front of my residence, Sugandh opened the door and right behind her, I saw Prabhat standing. Sugandh was blocking the way of my car with her both legs spread out and right hand at her waist. I smiled, and said, "Great! That is a really nice welcome. Come on kids, your daddy is home all tired and exhausted. Shouldn't you at least offer him a glass of water?" She looked at Prabhat and said, "Don't listen to anything he says today. Come on Prabhat, go sit in the car!" Prabhat rushed towards the car and sat in the front seat. Sugandh followed him and hopped in the back seat of the car. I knew that they feared that the ice-cream vendor might have already left. I said, "Kids! Ask your mummy to come along too, and then, close the main gate." Sugandh said, "Why don't you just start the engine?" She was worried that if her mummy came out before we left, she would never allow them to go out at 11 P.M. to have ice-cream.

The three of us hung around in the neighborhood till 12 A.M. and then, came back home. We kept chatting till 1 A.M., and then, went to sleep. Next day, Sunday morning, at 7 A.M., I was woken up by Arun's call. I recalled that I hadn't followed up with Aniruddh last night about his condition. Arun sounded very happy. He said, "Thanks, my son is alright. Now, I don't have to leave Oman in a hurry." I told him, "It is nearly time for my morning OPD. I will be done by 10.30 A.M. Ask Aniruddh to get the names of the medicines from me that will suffice up till tomorrow evening…and because it's Sunday today, I'll examine him tomorrow at East West Medical Center, Greater Kailash at 4 P.M. tomorrow. It's close to his place."

I got into my usual hectic schedule soon after attending the call. At 8 in the morning, I got bust with my patients in my home clinic. At around 10.30 AM, I found Sugandh and Prabhat sitting on sofa in our living room, watching morning shows on TV. I went ahead and sat down between them. The mobile rang again. It was Aniruddh on the line. "Yes, dear! Start taking those medicines and carry on until tomorrow evening, I will tell you about the further course of treatment tomorrow. Sugandh suffers from the same problem. She also takes the same medicine," I said. He replied, "I don't ride my motorbike during this season because of this very fear. I even avoid talking to my friends." "Very good boy!" I assured him and hung up. I looked at Sugandh and told her, "See, he is a grown-up boy but still he doesn't mind following every piece of advice. And you keep chatting the whole day on your mobile and roam around carrying doodle in your arms." She laughed aloud looking at Prabhat and said, "Dr. Ashok Sharma is the most cowardly man on earth. There is no such illness that prohibits you from speaking with others or roaming around, and Daddy, I didn't even sneeze once during the whole season." I turned their attention back to the TV program and quietly left for hospital.

I didn't even realize amidst the hustle bustle of the day how swiftly the weekend got over. While in my hospital round at 9.30 P.M., it struck me that having been so immersed in my work, I had totally forgotten about God. Just about a month ago, people from the nearby colony had collected some money and built a temple. The same month,I had made Sugandh install an idol of Goddess Saraswati in it. That was my only contribution. While directing the puja, the priest had said, "Doctor Sahab, it is not merely an idol of the Goddess, it is your third child. Now, it becomes your duty to serve her all your life. Your responsibility doesn't end with its installation, please don't forget that!" I reassured him, saying, "We will take care of her properly, and I will visit her every Sunday with family." I was quite annoyed with myself when I recalled all that. "Oh! It took us just a month to forget God." I thought, "It was nearly 10P.M. and if I go back home to pick up others, it would be too late. The temple might already be shut by the time we reach there." So, I asked my driver Sushil to turn the car towards the temple.

While sitting in the car, my thoughts wandered towards Diwakar, who had been working as a compounder in my clinic for the last 15 years and lived just opposite the temple and who would rush out to meet us whenever he noticed our car. I dialed

Diwakar's number. Luckily, he was at home. I told him, "I am reaching the temple in 5 minutes." It was sufficient for him to understand my implication. When the car reached the temple, he was already there waiting for me at the main gate. I looked at my watch; it was exactly 5 past 10. The lights around the temple had already been turned off. I called out for the priest without caring to take off my shoes or washing my hands. I just wanted to confirm that the temple had been closed for the day. The priest rushed out running towards me. Luckily, the priest, who was on duty in the service of God that day turned out to be my patient and hence, knew me very well. He said, "Why are you standing there? Doctor Sahab, please come on in. This temple can be closed for everyone but not for you." I said, "Panditji, all are equal in front of God. Please do not disturb God by switching on the temple lights just for me. I will pay my respects from outside." Panditji didn't seem to like the idea, and said, "Take off your shoes, come in and see for yourself." Then, he rushed back inside the temple. When I entered the temple with Diwakar,

I was surprised to see that Goddess Saraswati's, Goddess Durga's and Sai Baba's rooms were shut but the doors of Ram Darbar located in the middle of the temple were wide open, and a lamp was burning there, Panditji said, "The whole Darbar is waiting for you. Now, even God knows what a busy person you are. You are always busy taking care of your poor patients and it's really difficult for you to come to meet God." He put a teeka on my forehead and placed a laddu in my palm as prasadam. We came out of the temple. Diwakar said, "Please come to my place. You are free today earlier than usual after a long time. Let's have some tea." I said, "No, everybody must be waiting at home. It's Sunday today but it's already 10.30 P.M." On hearing this, Sushil turned the car homewards on his own. I was so happy that day. I took myself to be the greatest man in the world after what Panditji said. I reached home quickly. Usually, I hand over prasadam to my wife and she distributes it among everybody. But that day, along with that laddoo as prasadam, I rushed to my parents' room and told my mother, "Mom, a wonderful thing happened today. Panditji told me that now even god knows how busy a person I am. He doesn't go to sleep without meeting me." Then, without wasting any time at all, I gave every family member a little bit of the prasadam and rushed to Sugandh's room. I gave her the remaining half laddoo and said, "It is all yours. I have already distributed a little of it to the rest of the people."

It was 11 P.M. Every body went back to their rooms to sleep. I, too, went to my room very pleased. After watching news of the day on TV, I didn't realize when I went into a deep sleep. I suddenly woke up at 3.30 A.M. when I found a highly worried Prabhat shaking me vigorously and saying in a hurried voice, "Daddy, come downstairs fast. Sugandh is having an asthma attack." On reaching downstairs, I found that Sugandh was using the asthma machine called nebulizer and her breathing was shallow and long. Seeing this, I said, "You are using the nebulizer meant for patients. Where is your personal one, the one I got for you from abroad?"

"Daddy! I've not needed to use that in the past five years. I don't know where it is now. This machine is not helping me at all." I dialed my assistant Sarvar Khan's number immediately and he didn't take long to pick up. I asked him, "Which type of nebulizer is it? Sugandh is having trouble breathing and it's not working at all." He said, "Sir, it is by the company Amron,and it is totally new. Sir, I will be right there." I said, "Why would you come here? Rather, reach the nursing home, I am bringing her there." It looked as if an earthquake had hit our home. Prabhat ran and opened the door, Uma rushed outside to ask the by-lane guard to open the main gate, and I didn't waste any time in taking the car out. Uma lifted Sugandh in her arms, ran up to the car and dropped her in the backseat. My mom and dad remained asleep in their room. The servant of the house, Santu, who used to live in the servant quarters with his family, remained asleep but the pet Labradog Doodle that Sugandh had brought home only two months ago and whom she loved more than her own life, became restless. Struggling to breathe, Sugandh said to Prabhat, "Take her in, else she will run away." I said to Prabhat, "Sugandh didn't get any relief with Asthalin. We will administer Budicort to her in the Nursing Home and come back in ten minutes." Since driver was not on duty at 3 o' clock in the night, my hands were on the steering wheel. Without wasting any time, I began giving instructions to my Resident Doctor. The nursing home was only 3 kilometers away but the distance felt no less than 30 kilometers to me. Sugandh was now breathing more rapidly. I was yelling on mobile, "Be ready! Be ready! Oxygen, nebulizer, I.V. drip, emergency tray, one efcorlin injection…" The car was at the hospital gate in 2 minutes.

The nursing hostel of the hospital was upstairs. The Resident Doctor was waiting with 5-6 staff nurses, all prepared.

Emergency system was started as soon as Sugandh was laid down on the bed. The 8-10 injections that I had prescribed few minutes ago had already been given to her. Sugandh's condition was getting from bad to worse. She was begging for her life. Nearby, there was another well-reputed hospital. I used to visit it too as an expert. I told Uma, "She needs ventilator support. Let's shift her to Max immediately." By that time, Sarvar had also reached there. The whole staff got together and without removing the drip and oxygen, they placed Sugandh in the car and we rushed towards Max. I alerted the emergency staff of Max again through mobile. There again, the whole staff leapt into action to save Sugandh's life.

Whatever knowledge I had acquired about the true nature of asthma in the last 25 years, its essence was there in front of my eyes. The rapid up and down of data in the ICU monitor wastelling me in no unclear terms that it was not possible for even God to save Sugandh's life. I came out of the ICU and started crying, banging my head at the feet of Balaji Hanuman's idol kept at the reception; and then, I pleaded to God for the last time to save Sugandh's life. Just then, the mobile phone rang. It was Prabhat's call. He asked with great faith, "Is Sugandh alright now?" Crying, I said, "No, son! She is very critical. Pray to God." I was aware that Sugandh had already left us. The procedures in the

ICU were mere formalities. I lost my composure. My friends kept asking me repeatedly, "What did Sugandh eat last night?" They suspected that it was an allergic reaction of some food. I was yelling at the top of my voice, "She had eaten prasadam from the temple. How can someone die after consuming prasadam? It has the power to revive the dead."

Now, I was faced with the huge dilemma of breaking the bad news to Prabhat. How should I tell him? Meanwhile, Prabhat woke up Arora aunty, borrowed her car and left for the hospital to visit Sugandh. My friend brought me home in his car. All of this happened in a span of just half an hour.

The news spread like wild fire. By morning, a large number of people had gathered in the by-lane. The nursing staff, college students, all teachers, well-known people of the city, everyone had tear-filled eyes. This sudden unbelievable death had caused fear in everyone present there and it was quite evident from their faces. Even little kids were angry with God. Some people were so angry that they tore pictures of God. Their contention was that if God could treat a God-like person in this manner, then He doesn't exist. I didn't even realize how 3-4 hours passed in shedding tears. By noon, Sugandh's body had reached the crematorium by hearse for her last rites. The priest was ready with her funeral pyre. She was surrounded only by Prabhat,I and a few distinguished people of the city about whom I had the notion that when they were around, nothing was impossible to achieve in this world, and these same people were standing quietly, with their heads hanging down, looking totally helpless.

I was standing in front of Sugandh's pyre, with folded hands, asking for forgiveness. I was saying, "Sugandh, please forgive me. I provided you with all the luxuries of life but the time that I should have spent with you went in serving the patients. I never attended any of your sports days, annual days, parents' meetings, and annual functions because I spent that time in conducting free camps and emergency services." I had the feeling that Prabhat and I were the only one there. Once the last rites were over, the priest gathered every one and announced that starting today, three days later, family members would visit the crematorium again and collect Sugandh's remains and immerse them in the Ganges. That will be the only last puja performed for her. I was shocked. I reacted sharply, "We won't be in mourning for 12 days? We won't offer meals to a Brahmin every month?" The priest replied, "All these are prohibited for unmarried girls." I started crying inconsolably. I said, "Wonderful! Panditji, that is fantastic. I had the impression that discrimination between girls and boys was limited to birth but now I find that you people continue this discrimination even after death." And then I made up my mind that I would sleep on the floor for a month, would offer meals to a young girl every month, and on the first anniversary of Sugandh's death, I would observe her first *tithi* in Hardwar. Relatives, brothers and sisters, consoled us and all left after 3rd-4th day. Now, there were only three of us in the house and only Doodle was there to console us. Many patients would visit the clinic every day but they would console me and leave on seeing my mental state.

They would forget their own illnesses. A week passed. I was not able to make myself attend to the patients. But the large crowd of patients waiting outside for a week was slowly losing patience. They would ask Sarvar and Madam repeatedly – "Why isn't Doctor Sahab attending to us? What is our fault? Our whole family has been availing treatment only from him for the last 20 years. Where would we go, now?" Madam came to my bedroom, and said, "Why don't you attend to them?" I said, "I have been serving these very people for the last 20 years. I have never had any time for my own family. I had so much faith in God, I used to believe that my family could never come to any harm because I had entrusted the welfare of my whole family to God's own care. God has cheated me. He made me dedicate 20 years of my life to the service of both *nar and narayan* (man and God) and in return, he has handed me the corpse of my little girl.You know, I can't even commit suicide because one takes his own life when he is cheated by a human. I have been cheated by God himself. Now, I have made up my mind, I will never indulge myself in any religious activity." Madam said, "Fine, so that's how much you hate God now? OK, but you can't deny that you loved Sugandh very much. So, don't attend to these patients for the sake of God, attend to them for the sake of Sugandh. You know, why? Because these people waiting outside, are saying, 'Doctor Sahab is a very good man, but now he will become worthless.' And Sugandh will be held responsible for that." I wiped my tears quickly, went into the clinic and began attending to my patients.

At home, Uma had begun *pitridosh* puja that would go on for 10 days. There were no tears in her eyes. She would keep the religious channel on TV running throughout the day and listening to the religious teachings. She had finished studying *Gita* and was always occupied with performing some kind of *puja* in front of Sugandh's picture after consulting *Panditji*. The living room had begun to look like a temple. Prabhat had grown quiet. It seemed as if he had taken the vow of silence. He would respond only in 'yes' and 'no'. My parents would not leave any opportunity to console the three of us and they had grown more restless and anxious.

Both of them were heart patients. Father had bypass surgery done. We were clueless about how to take care of everyone in the family. Gradually, a month passed in mourning and shedding tears. My parents moved to my elder brother's place. Prabhat would attend school occasionally and at other times, would pretend to have a headache and remain asleep in his room. In order to improve his emotional state, his school's principal and teachers recommended that we should take him to a religious place. We left for a visit to the Salasar Balaji temple located in Rajasthan. I bowed my head down in front of Salasar Maharaj and folding my hands, I said, "Oh God, every time we paid you a visit, there would be four of us, then, why are there only three people this time? Now, I will be back only when there are four of us again. Kindly accept my regards." Within fifteen days of this visit, Sarvar Khan took us to Ajmer Shareef Dargah. Since then, we would spend every weekend at some temple or a religious place. When we visited Hanuman temple, Uma in a rebuking voice said, "I have noticed that you have stopped taking God's *Arti* and offering flowers."

I said, "My faith in God is stronger now. Only those people offer flowers and money that are happy. You want me too to offer the same and say, 'Thanks God! You have done a great job.'? I have been wronged and I am not the only one to say so. Every child in this colony feels the same about God now. Hence, I will visit every temple with you and complain to every God about it."

The mention of God reminded me of the Brij–Vihar temple which I had visited a few hours before Sugandh's death; the same temple where I had made Sugandh install the Saraswati idol; the same temple which I had vowed to visit every Sunday. I got into my car and drove straight to it. I was there after three months. People of Brij–Vihar and the priest of the temple were sure that Doctor Sahab has lost faith in God and he would not show any interest in the temple-related activities anymore.I stopped outside Ram Darbar in the temple and started crying inconsolably in front of God. Everyone came in and stood behind me. I had just one question to God, "Why did I find you awake that night? Had I found you covered like others, I would have known that it was an unlucky day for me. Since I was late, I lost the opportunity of meeting you. You showed up and made the priest say that you had been waiting for me. Were you waiting for me so that you could give me that prasadam that Sugandh ate and finally lost her life? You haven't punished me; you have punished all these people. All these poor people made efforts to collect some money and got this temple built. Each of them pays 10 rupees every month, each of them helps in paying the priest's salary and electricity bill. It has just been one and a half months since this temple opened. Now, all these people are scared of you. They are scared of bringing their children with them to this temple. After listening to my words, the priest came forward, and after showing some compassion, gave me the prasadam. I accepted it and said to him, "Your prasadam cost me so much. I will not take it home. I will consume it myself in front of this God." I ate it right there and drove back home. Next day, my friend Dr. Wagnoo, who was a doctor in the Apollo hospital and way older than me said, "Why are you stuck with the same theory? You used to visit the temple on regular basis and take prasadam. It was merely a coincidence that the accident took place that day." I said, "How can I accept that? What do you mean by coincidence? What all do you want me to forget as mere coincidence? Why did Arun call me the same night? Why did he call me, in particular? He could have called up some other class-fellow of mine. Why did his son have an asthma attack the very same day? He could have had a cough, fever, cold or any other problem. Do you think all this was mere coincidence? Just watch, I will certainly get my answers some day from God."

Six months had passed since Sugandh's death. Diwali was round the corner. I was at home. My servant Santu came running and said, "A gentleman in a car with red lights has come to see you." As I got up to see who it was, I found the former Election Commissioner Doctor G.V.G. Krishnamurthy walking in. I considered him my Guru and a father figure. On seeing me, he said, "Hey you! We are old and helpless people. You used to visit us every Sunday to enquire about my health. But you haven't visited us at all in the last three months. I have come here today to cheer you all up. After settling down in the living room, he said, "What are your plans for Diwali?" I said, "We will never celebrate Diwali. The Goddess Lakshmi of our house became upset with us and has left us forever. So, we will spend our Diwali sitting in some temple." He said, "Fine, let me arrange a visit for all of you to Tirupati Balaji on Diwali." We reached Tirupati Balaji on Diwali by air. Mr. Royal, the secretary of the management committee, took us inside the temple through the VIP route. When we came out of the temple after paying our respects, I noticed that Prabhat looked better. He was in tenth grade and had his board exams that year. After Sugnadha's death, his performance at school had been deteriorating with each passing day. He was getting only 24 out of 80 marks or 18 out of 60 marks in one test or another. On being asked, he would say, "I leave the examination paper blank. I just can't recall anything that I study." Hence, I thought he must have prayed for something related to studies. I asked him, "What did you pray to God for?" He just uttered a single word, "Moksha". I asked, "Now, what is that?" He replied, "I don't know. Mom keeps saying that Sugandh has achieved Moksha. So, I asked for the same from God for three of us." Tears trickled down my eyes. Ignoring them, I asked Uma, "And what did you ask for?" She said, "The same thing that I ask for every day." I continued, "What?" She replied, "Moksha for Sugandh." Right then, the driver of the car appeared and said, "Sahab, did you visit the temple?" I said, "Yes. We were entitled for a VIP visit. So, it didn't take us long to complete our visit." The driver said, "Sahab, if you allow me, I would like to stand in the general queue and have a *darshan* of Balaji. It would take me about 8 hours." I said, "Of course, go ahead. Take your time. We will leave tomorrow."

In the meantime, Prabhat and Uma had started walking slowly towards the room. I began to think, "How would I spend the next 8-9 hours sitting in the room? I will keep thinking about what Prabhat and Uma said and worry myself unnecessarily. It would be better if I joined the driver in the queue and visited Balaji once again." On reaching the door of the temple, it struck me, "How can I go in? I had said to God barely an hour ago, 'This is my first and last visit to you. Kindly forgive me if I committed any sin in this lifetime. It is probable that I may never visit you again.'" The moment I recalled all this, I said to the driver, "You may go in. I will wait outside." Once the driver left, I began to cry. Here, I could cry to my heart's content. I couldn't cry in the room in front of Prabhat and Uma. While shedding tears, I pleaded to God, "Oh, God! Please have mercy on this child. He has no idea what *Moksha* is. But he is asking for *Moksha* from you, and Uma is also at fault. How can you give *Moksha* to a 17-18 year old girl? You grace someone with *Moksha* only when that person dedicates his complete life to your service, because as much as I know about spirituality, it is only when one has achieved satisfaction in this world, he or she can aspire to achieve *Moksha*. I just don't understand the desire of achieving *Moksha* at such an early age! If you wish me to serve you, you shall have to give me back my daughter. Through her, I will immerse myself in the service of *Nar* and *Narayan* and also, please make me so capable that I am able to fulfil each and every wish that my daughter makes." Then, we left Tirupati and returned to Delhi.

These days, minor *pujas* had become a daily affair. Sometimes *pujas* would be held on the occasion of *Amavasya* (new moon) and sometimes on the occasion of *Ekadashi* (special puja on the eleventh day of lunar cycle). Once the puja was over, the priest would ask me," How do you feel now? Do you feel relaxed?" I would reply, "*Panditji*, earlier, I used to perform puja out of heart-felt love for God. With a lot of enthusiasm, I would collect garlands, fruits, etc. and would make sure that everything was perfect. But now, I perform puja out of fear, and my hands shake when I go through the rituals in front of God. A fear keeps gnawing away at me, 'What if I make a mistake and God punishes me for that!'

PART II

Gradually, my dream house, my little paradise, completely turned into hell. Earlier, the loud western music playing on deck in Sugandh's room used to announce her presence in the house even before one had stepped inside. But now, the way she used to run up and down the stairs with Doodle, laugh aloud with Prabhat while discussing the mischiefs done in school, and cuss friends on mobile, all seemed like a dream.

Uma had transformed herself into an absolute ascetic. She would be teary-eyed only when someone visited to mourn on Sugandh's death. She would spend her day reading some or other religious book. Every TV set and every music system was covered in layers of dust. Only the TV set placed in the living room kept playing Bhagwat, sponsored by a certain religious channel, all day long.

Prabhat would spend all his time in his room. He had also cut down on his eating. Every evening, instead of going out to play, he would take out his cycle and visit the temple. The temple priest had become quite friendly with him.

One day, I asked the priest, "What does he ask for from God?" He said, "He keeps asking when my father would become his usual self again?" On hearing this, I told him, "Pandit ji, now, even if your God wishes, it is impossible for him to make me the way I used to be."

Far off in Ajmer, my 83-year old father had been admitted to hospital four times in the last five months. Earlier, whenever he used to fall ill, I would rush to meet him and bring him along to Delhi but now, I had lost the spirit to do the same. I could no longer extend any medical advice to any of my family members.

One day unexpectedly, I got a call from the Red Cross hospital. They had an urgent requirement of a part-time Pathologist. Uma used to work there fifteen years ago. She had resigned from this post after Prabhat's birth keeping in mind her increased familial responsibilities.

I got Uma to take up the job immediately. I believed that it would make her spend some time outside the house. At home, I had arranged for tuition classes in Physics and Mathematics for

Prabhat to keep him occupied. Everyone would say, "Keep Prabhat happy, he should mean everything to you now."

I was stuck in a strange dilemma. Keep your patients happy, keep your parents happy, keep Prabhat happy, and for keeping all these people happy, I had to keep myself happy, which was totally impossible. I had nothing left but agony. How could I spread happiness? And I didn't want to share my grief with anyone. I wanted to remain immersed in it. Whenever I got time alone, I would weep to my heart's content. Hospital's car parking, the washroom at home, and the tiny temple at home were my favorite places for shedding tears. Every day, I would cry and open my heart to God. I would say, "You gave me such colossal grief, and you ask me to stop crying, to keep working? From now on, I will cry in front of you only."

But nothing could stop the flow of tears now. My eyes were always full to the brim with them. Tears would flow countless times during the day. I would wipe my eyes before leaving for a round of the ward and would appear normal in front of the patients but once I would be out of the ward and come across a familiar face, I would be teary-eyed again. I was aware that if I met a doctor or a relative of any patient, they would ask me about my well-being. Then, I would become tongue-tied, and my tears would give the reply. All the anatomy and physiology books of my student days would tell how much blood the body makes in a day, and how much water it expels daily. But none of the books said anything about tears. A tear is merely a product of the lacrimal gland, which is as small as a Bengal gram. This gland can hold only as much tears that a hungry child needs to cry and wake up its mother. But it seemed that I possessed a never-ending supply of tears. Whenever this gland would be exhausted, I would be reminded of Sugandh's lively face, and then, I would lose myself in her thoughts. People say, 'The one whose time has come gets a premonition of his/her death.' The same had happened around the time Sugandh died. While on the way to the hospital, I would sit in the backseat of the car wearing black goggles and would lose myself in the events of my past. These black goggles would hide the tears that would flow while recalling Sugandh's past. Six months prior to her death, she had become a different person. She had developed a carefree attitude towards her future and she would never worry about her studies. She would dare to go to PVR and watch the newly-released movie just before the day of her exams. Yes, she would not get good scores, she would just scrape though her exams. Since her early days, she had been more inclined towards new music albums, fashion, etc. She would paint in her leisure time. She would never step into the kitchen. She would not even go in for a glass of water and would rather ask the servant to bring it to her room. A few days before her death, I noticed that Sugandh had bought milk powder Cerelac from the store and was eating it. I burst into laughter and said, "What are you up to Sugandh? When you were a little kid and your mom would feed you milk forcibly, you used to cry so much that people in the neighborhood would come to know that Sugandh was having milk. And now you are having baby food after returning from college? People would make fun of you dear!

She laughed and said, "Daddy, it is so tasty, why don't you also try?" and saying this, she fed me also a spoonful of the milk powder. Now, after 6 months of that incident, I knew why she had been eating Cerelac powder. Perhaps she had begun to prepare herself for her next life! Probably, during the last few days of her life, she had realized that she did not have much time left. She had suddenly become very ambitious. She had joined coaching classes for CAT exams. She had also taken admission in the part time French language course in YMCA. She even had visited the NOIDA film city and gave an interview for radio jockeying. As if she was in a hurry to do everything, without missing out on anything in life, anymore. I would keep mulling over these things and my journey from the hospital to home would get over in the blink of an eye.

Today, I had to visit East West Medical Center, GK-1. It used to take exactly an hour to reach that place. Earlier, there used to be piles of medical journals and books in the back seat of my car, and the moment the driver would start the car engine, I would immerse myself in my studies. But now, those books were all covered with layers of dust. I did not touch them anymore. I had started believing that these books contained nothing but lies. They said that asthma was completely treatable. And, it was something that I could not accept at all, anymore.

Now, while in the car, I neither read nor talked to anyone on mobile. I just loved to wear my black glasses and peep into my past. Today, I remembered the Sunday just before Sugandh's death. That afternoon when I entered the house, I saw Uma scolding her. I asked her, "Why are you scolding her? Come on! Sugandh is going to be here only for a few more days. Then, she will leave for hostel for her IIPM studies. And then, God knows, she might get married any time or go away with a job. Who knows? Treat her like a guest in this house." Uma replied, "I can't help it, I have to scold her!" Then, pointing at Sugandh, she continued, "Madam is insisting on going to mall with her friends. And now, she has begun to backchat too. She says, 'I will get even with you in my next birth!'" I said, "Why dear? Why did you say that?" Sugandh replied, "Yes, I did say that. I would become the mother of you two." I said, "How can it happen? Do you mean Uma and I would be siblings? But the relationship between husband and wife is meant to last for 7 life times." Sugandh said, "No, and I will teach both of you the best way of living life. I couldn't correct you people in this life time. Both of you have spent away your life looking after patients and visiting hospitals, and you have failed to see the world." I said, "But how would you correct us? Tell me." Sugandh said, "At the age of 3, I will take both of you to malls and feed ice creams." I replied, "I don't want such kind of life. A mother like you will not provide us with any education and when we would grow up, we would curse our mother that she did not pay any attention to our studies." Saying this, I started laughing. And the memory of that laugh made me cry in the car. It brought me back to reality tearing me away from my past. Now, the thought that Sugandh had a hunch of her death made me upset. Why didn't we have any such premonition? Did she really have an inkling of her imminent death?

Khatu Shyamji, Balaji, Tirupati Balaji, Ajmer Shareef, Bangla Sahib Gurudwara, Manasa Devi, Kul Devi in Mathura – hardly any religious place was left where I had not paid a visit and narrated my sorrowful tale.

It was nearly a year since Sugandh had left us. I was increasingly getting worried about Prabhat – 'He has his tenth grade board exams this year. What if out of nervousness, he leaves the exam sheets blank? How would he spend 3-month long vacations following the exams?' Prabhat and Sugandh had spent the previous year's summer holidays in their maternal aunt's house in Australia. The moment I recalled it, I dialed Sydney's number and soon, Prabhat's uncle was on the line. I told him, "I am unable to keep Prabhat happy. Now, this is your testing time. Once his exams are over, I will send him to Australia along with Uma. If he likes the place, get him an admission over there in the next session in eleventh grade. In five-six years, when his studies are over, I would also move to Australia for good." He was very happy to hear this and said, "I have been suggesting you the same for the last one year. You too immediately move over here. Everything will be alright."

We went to Hardwar to celebrate Sugandh's first death anniversary. Kumbh bath was being held during those days. After performing *puja*, Uma was sure that Sugandh had attained Moksha. However, I kept on believing that Sugandh would return to this world. Sugandh's picture that was kept in our home had not been adorned yet with a garland. Uma and Prabhat left for Sydney a day later. Our servant Santu moved into our house along with his mother, wife Savita and child. But I was all alone. I had only two tasks now. The first was to treat my patients, and the second was to cry my heart out in front of God.

'Oh God! Since the moment you created this universe, you have been teaching the human race that truth always conquers everything. But I don't understand why you resort to violence to teach us this lesson. During the Mahabharata age, innumerable innocent soldiers from both sides had to sacrifice their lives to prove the righteousness of just 5 Pandavas. The same had happened during the Rama-Ravana battle. It led to the burning down of Golden Lanka into ashes. You have nearly shackled me in your sorcery also. Every single day, I am responsible for the lives of at least 100 patients, and they expect a lot from me. They consider me an incarnation of God. These people with child-like innocence sitting outside believe that once they reach my cabin, all of their sorrow and pain will vanish.

But now, I have made up my mind, I will not let these poor people get affected by the ongoing conflict between you and me. I will treat them with the best of my ability and I will not let them die. And if I fail to do the same, I will go away to some far off place leaving all these people to your mercy.

Prabhat's tenth grade results had been declared. He had performed far better than expected and had secured 92% marks. Soon, I got a call from his uncle. Sounding very upset, he said, "I am sending Uma and Prabhat back to India. Prabhat needs his father. He is not ready to live here without you." I was aware that it was impossible for me to move to Australia. I had never even planned to apply for a visa, and even if I had got it somehow, how could I've met the expenses over there without working?

Three days later, they returned to Delhi. Prabhat was glad to see his marks. It was not as if our household was the only one where there was anger against God. Outside too, people had lost their composure. Some people had torn down pictures of God. Mr. Gupta, who used to deal in *khoya* in Chandni Chowk, had banged his head so severely on the temple stairs that one could see the marks on his forehead to that day. Babu Khan Sahab, who used to work in the police department, had gone as far as mentally preparing his 14-year old daughter, "If doctor Uncle does not get well, I will send you forever to his house." Most elderly women would say, "Oh! I wish God had taken my life instead!" I would hear people saying, "Our Doctor Sahab was a very good man but God has been cruel to him." I didn't like it when people criticized God. One person would sit at the temple door, another would remain in a corner in the mosque, and then another one would offer prayers at the Gurdwara while someone else would remain seated in the church. Together, all these people shook the power we call God.

And it worked. Like magic, God began to give us signs of him being happy with us. Prabhat started going out to watch IPL matches and focusing on his eleventh grade studies. I brought back my father from Ajmer to Delhi and began his treatment. He completely regained his health, and the incident that transpired next, was totally beyond anyone's imagination. There was a seemingly impossible job and God entrusted me with the responsibility of completing it.

Broadly speaking, there were phone numbers of more than 200 Sugandh's friends stored on her mobile. A few of them had called back and asked about the cause of her death. Some of her friends had cried a lot while some had ended the call with just an 'Okay'. They had not bothered to ask about the cause of her death.

Parul was Sugandh's closest friend. She used to live nearby and was Ms. Prabha Sharma's daughter, who used to work with IFCI. Parul had been studying with Sugandh since sixth grade and visiting our house every day to play with Prabhat and Sugandh.

One day, Parul called up. She said, "Uncle, Parul speaking."

I asked her, "What are you busy with these days?"

She said, "Uncle, I am doing B.Sc. Microbiology from Coimbatore. I am in Faridabad right now for summer holidays. I need to see you…and Uncle, there is something very important that I would like to discuss with you."

I told her, "Now, you are Sugandh for me. Come over, this house belongs to you."

Parul arrived and said, "Uncle…Uncle, Sugandh is about to return."

Uma and I were stunned to hear that, and we could not take our eyes off her face. Her eyes were shining and she was speaking with great confidence, "Aunty, Sugandh often appears in my dreams. In her earlier appearances, she used to have a dull look on her face. Her hair used to be unkempt. She would not utter a single word. She would only cry over my shoulder. I never breathed a word to you all about it for the last one year because I feared that it would only make you sadder. But, you know, she was the tom boy of my class. This time she appeared in her usual style, wearing jeans, and said to me, "Oh buddy, come on now, stop crying, I will return shortly." On hearing that, I went near Parul and urged her, "Dear, why did you fall silent? Tell us everything Sugandh does."

Parul said, "She helps us a lot. That's all. I can't tell you anything more."

I said, "Dear, please keep our telephone numbers and do let us know if she asks for something in your dreams."

Parul left leaving me sleepless at night. I could see a little glimmer of hope in the absolute darkness. A few days later, Prabhaji visited my clinic for a checkup and said, "Doctor Sahab, start looking for Sugandh...other children are also saying things like Parul is."

I said, "Prabhaji, what are you talking about? It is impossible. She didn't get lost in a fair or anything... where should I look for her? It is not possible for anyone to come back from the place she went, and even if she returns to this world, we won't be able to recognize her anymore. Who knows where she would be born and what she would look like?"

Prabhaji said, "Shailja told me that Sugandh appeared in her dream in school dress. She was standing in her living room and said, "Shailja, look, here I am." Shailja continued, "Crazy girl, you cannot come back." Sugandh said, "Shailja, come on, touch me…my white scooty is parked outside." Little drops of sweat appeared on my forehead on hearing these words. Nobody knew about the white scooty except Sugandh and me. A few days before her death, she had asked me to get her a white scooty. I had told her, "Nowadays, kids start asking for scooty the moment they enter university. Neither do they hold a permanent driving license nor do they know how to drive properly. They cause accidents nearly every day and break their bones. I see this nonsense all the time in my hospital. Often, I see poor parents pleading anxiously to the police officials. So, I will never get you a scooty while you are studying in the university. You will get a car once you are a graduate." Sugandh had left with a smile after hearing my decision.

But now, Shailja's dream had given me a new lease of life. I ran to Prabhat and Uma, and narrated the same dream to them. Prabhat was glad to hear it but Uma broke into such a realistic speech that my enthusiasm died down in a few minutes. Uma used to place utmost importance to preforming her duties. Emotions had no place in her life. She explained to me, "Doctor Ashok Sharma, come out of your dream world. Fulfill your responsibilities. You are a mature doctor. Your son is not paying attention to his studies, he is not eating properly. Take care of him. Your parents are not well, look after them. Your behavior is a cause of concern to your patients. They keep wondering anxiously, 'When would our Doctor Sahab overcome this grief and look after us like he used to do in earlier.'"

On hearing her words, tears began to trickle down my eyes. I said, "Who am I to take care of Prabhat? Only your God can fulfil this task. You keep saying that if the child did good deeds in his past life, he would be happy in this one. Your God has pre-decided how long my parents would live, and as for the patients, how can the doctor, who couldn't save his own daughter, be expected to save their lives?"

Saying this, I came out of the room but I had become restless. I started feeling that Sugandh was somewhere very close to me and she was crying out to me through her friends, "Daddy, please call me back." I sat down in front of her photo and began to weep. With folded hands, I pleaded to her photo hanging to the wall, "Dear, please come back. See how distressed Prabhat and I are. We just can't live without you. You had the knack of getting your way with your teachers. You can bring around God too." I couldn't sleep the whole night. The wish to get back Sugandh had now turned into an obsession.

I spent a sleepless night. Next morning, I finished the morning OPD and went to a music store. I bought a few CDs of old Hindi films based on rebirth and began watching them. Uma was not impressed by all that. She told me that all those were imaginary stories. They were meant to entertain people. But her opinion could not discourage me.

I was seeking my goal and I put rigorous efforts to find it. Next day, I went to a bookstore and noticed certain books written by the famous psychiatrist Brian Weiss. I bought his two books, The Masters of Universe and Many Souls Many Bodies, and finished reading them the same night.

The reading of these two books restored my lost confidence. I began to feel that it was possible for Sugandh to come back. I started thinking of bringing her back with the help of medical science. It was a difficult task but not an impossible one. Uma had already gone through two major surgeries. She was 46 years old. Motherhood at this age is quite common in the western countries but in ours, most women prepare themselves to become grandmothers.

I presented my idea to my senior friends. Dr. Wagnoo was not only my friend but my Guru too. He was the Head of Department of Endocrinology and medical advisor to the President as well. When I told him my intent, he said, "I have been trying to make you see this point for the last one year. Today, you have uttered my heart's intent on your own. In our culture, parents live solely for making their kids happy. They are ready to go to any length for ensuring their child's happiness. We have to anyhow make Prabhat happy. He is only 15 years old, and he has a long life ahead of him. How would he move on with his life if he has to carry the burden of his sister's loss in his life? I will discuss your case with the best lady doctors. If God wills, Prabhat will get his sister back."

When I told all that to Uma, she burst into fit of rage. She said, "Your friends and you have lost your mind over a few dreams seen by kids. Has anyone ever returned from that place?"

I was fully prepared to respond aptly to all her arguments that day. I replied, "Yes! Some people have definitely come back. Satyavan came back, and Savitri brought him back. I had no knowledge of it, I found their mention in your books only. The love that exists between Sugandh and I is far deeper than the love that Savitri and Satyavan had between them. I will certainly prove this truth to your God."

Uma relented a little and said in a very humble voice, "I have noticed how restless you have been in the last few days. I also want Sugandh to come back but the method that you all are using is wrong. It is impossible to become a mother at this age, and it is all the more difficult to bring up children. Only a woman can understand it. You men will never understand. I also have a solution for this problem." Saying this, she threw an envelope towards me. The envelope carried my horoscope that she had taken to an astrologer for a reading.

The astrologer had asked, "Madam, whose horoscope is it?"

Uma: My husband's.

Astrologer: What do you want to know?

Without any introduction, Uma had directly asked, "Do you see any probability of his second marriage?"

The astrologer stood up in his seat with a start. He said, "Madam, I bow down to you in the standing position. In my 30-year career, I never came across a lady, who brought her husband's horoscope to me with this purpose in mind."

"I am very worried. I wish that another woman would take over my household responsibilities letting me leave this house and the mundane world, and go to Haridwar."

Uma was ready to make a sacrifice that was far more magnanimous than what Dr. Wagnoo and I were contemplating to ask from her.

I said to her, "You are doing all this for Prabhat. But have you ever thought what would happen to him? He will never be able to live without you. He will never accept any other woman in your place, and he would never accept the child born from that woman as his brother/sister."

"God has shown us a new path and we will certainly take it. I agree that it's difficult to become a mother at your age, but we will take one step at a time. We will get all your tests done. I will give it a go ahead only if we find that you are physically and mentally fit to be a mother. Everything will be done under the care of the best doctors. I never wish that in the process of getting back his sister, Prabhat ends up losing his mother too." Uma was totally quiet now. She said, "Please give me some time to think about it." I said, "I will wait for the day when you would approach me on your own and say, 'I am ready to be a mother again.'" Uma advised me to pay a visit to Vaishno Devi. I immediately agreed. I said, "Yes, that's the only place where we should make our request."

Next weekend, I paid a visit to Vaishno Devi all alone. Time was short because I had dedicated all my time to my patients and I had to take out some time out of from what was completely meant for them.

It was heavily raining there. People had taken shelter in the resting places built here and there, and were waiting for the rain to stop but I kept walking as I had to catch the return flight the following day. I had to reach Katra by night after finishing my *darshan*. There were tears in my eyes. I was continuously chanting 'Jai Mata di, Jai Mata di'. As I covered a little distance, the rain abruptly stopped and I saw a man with a horse cart standing in front of me. It seemed as if he had been sent by Mata herself. He took only 2 hours to cover the distance of 11 kilometers to take me to Mata's *darbar*. I cried a lot in front of Mata. Everyone was singing and dancing. People looked very happy. I just stood before Mata with folded hands. I couldn't make any offering to her, neither flowers nor a coconut. I was begging for mercy, "Oh Mata, I am the only one here, who arrived with tears in his eyes. Please bless Uma and me both with so much strength that we come back to you with a smile on our faces."

After returning home, Uma urged me to meet the astrologer. He said, "Madam, as per your horoscope, your life is full of struggles, and it is meant to serve others. So, you cannot renounce the world and turn your back to your responsibilities. I do see the indication of an addition in your family, and this conjunction will last only for a year. True, I can't tell if it would be a boy or a girl but whatever may be the sex of the child, it would have a mole on its right shoulder. That's all I can tell you."

Two days later, Uma came and sitting down in front of me, said, "I can't bear to see your distressed face anymore. Take me to any lady doctor of your choice. I am ready but I would like you to know that my decision has nothing to do with your insistence. I made up my mind after asking my God for guidance and a thorough reading of *Shastras* (holy books)." I asked her, "And what did *Shastras* tell you in this regard?" "They say that it is the duty of the Indian woman to always support her husband in his struggle, and I am full-heartedly with you. But you know I have to fulfill my duties towards Prabhat as well. So, I will not go out of Delhi for my treatment." I was very happy to hear it. I thanked Vaishno Mata. It was undoubtedly no less than a miracle that Uma had finally given her approval,

I immediately called up Dr. Deeksha, Dr. Madhubhavini, and Dr. Gupta. They also found it very strange. Dr. Deeksha said, "In my 20-year career, I have never come across a case like this one. Usually, it is the woman, who keeps begging for a child. But here, I see the father begging for getting his daughter back and the mother opposing the idea."

All my doctor friends and lady doctors reassured Uma that all of us would try our best to bring back Sugandh into this world. I was successful in making a breakthrough. After being indecisive for six months, Uma, finally, had emotionally prepared herself for embracing motherhood.

Now, it remained to be seen if she was physically capable of becoming a mother at this age. What if she was suffering from diabetes or hypertension? A number of tests were performed, and all of them turned out encouraging. My faith in God was indeed getting stronger.

My parents, who had been living with us, had no inkling of what Uma and I were up to. We were being very secretive about everything, be it our visits with respect to the treatment or discussions over reports. Prabhat also was unaware of all these developments. My father would often explain to me, "Our grief won't last more than 2-3 years. We will get Prabhat married early and that will fill up the void that Sugandh's death has created in our family." I knew very well that they said all that to cheer me up. It would take another ten years to make all that happen. Prabhat was only 15 years old, and it would need another 2 years for his schooling to finish. After that, he would join the university and later on, take up a job. I had stopped making long-term plans for my child. We were not even sure of what might happen the next moment! I had envisaged many things for Sugandh. I had planned to marry her off with great fanfare. Every time. I had brought jewellery for Uma, she had immediately placed it in the locker for Sugandh saying it would be an asset for her. We had purchased a plot for building another hospital but we could never muster enough courage to start its construction. We had always wondered, 'If we use up all our money for this, how would we meet Sugandh's educational and marriage-related expenses?' But it took just a second to change all that. Now, all the items that we had slowly collected for her wedding, would make us terribly sad whenever we look at them.

It was Prabhat's eleventh grade half-yearly examination. He was as usual sad when he came back from school. I immediately realized that this time too, he could not perform well. Earlier, he would enter the house running and declare in his unique way that he would secure above 90%. Now, his nonchalant attitude while entering the house caused us anxiety and fear. We were very fearful that his poor performance might drive him to leave studies mid-way. With a worried voice, I asked, "What's wrong?" Weeping, he said, "The exam didn't go well."

I replied, "What's new? You never perform well in mathematics, because you aspire to get 100%."

Prabhat said, "I will not get full marks anyway. I left questions worth 20 marks."

I consoled him saying, "So what? You will get passing marks for sure." He had performed very well in other subjects. What went wrong today? Prabhat was not much of a talker. He said, "I couldn't sleep well last night. I am awake since 3 AM."

I asked, "Why?"

Prabhat replied, "I had a dream. I saw Sugandh again."

I asked him with great enthusiasm, "What was she doing?"

Prabhat said, "She was standing near the main door of the living room, close to the microwave. She said, "Hey, you just can't imagine, God made me pay so many visits!"

That was enough to shake me up. I leapt towards Prabhat and embraced him. I had tears of joy. I said, "Prabhat, it is a really big deal. God gave us a test and we are very close to passing that test with flying colors. This test is incomparable with the small man-made tests that you keep taking in your school. Now, I am very happy." Prabhat did not get me and I didn't want to divulge any detail to him. When I reiterated Prabhat's dream to Uma, she scolded me as always. She said, "You have made it a habit to live in the world of dreams. Rather, go to Prabhat's school and discuss his problem with his teacher." Paying no heed to her advice, I started living in the world of dreams. I had no doubt that there was another world, existing far off this world, and it had its own rules and regulations. Sugandh had said that she had paid innumerable visits. What kind of visits? Where did she pay these visits? All these questions were unanswered.

Physically, I was living in this world but my heart was living in the world of God. I could not share all these things with anyone. People would have called me insane. But I had become crazy for

God. I felt as if an invisible force was helping me. I would keep talking to God in the temple in my house.

Uma's IVF tests had begun. The doctor told us of 30% probability. I said, "I would carry on even if there was only 1% probability because if I don't, I will always be guilty of not giving my best in trying to bring back my daughter into this world." I would repeatedly say this to Sugandh's photo, "Dear, you have to come back into this world. You have to do this for Prabhat's sake. You have to do this for my sake. You have to come back into this world for the sake of these patients."

When I would take a break from these thoughts and become aware of the real world, I would become sad. The thought that Sugandh would return seemed impossible and far-fetched.

Just two days before Diwali, Uma gave me the good news. Her pregnancy test was positive. While telling me about it, she was not happy but fearful. And, she was right in many respects.

When Prabhat was born, her condition had become critical after the surgery. She had to be given blood transfusion. I encouraged her, saying. "I am not scared at all. God has lead us till this day, he will never leave us in a lurch. We will carry on with full faith in him." On Diwali, it seemed as if we were getting back our lost Lakshmi.

When we showed her report to Dr. Deeksha, she was in disbelief. She said, "This report is faulty. It can't happen so soon. Get a sonography done." The sonography report shocked all the doctors. As per their understanding, it was probable that there were twin children, and it was impossible to deliver twin children at this age. But I was not worried at all. I had absolute faith in God. I kept chanting God's name all the time. I asked Uma to take a lot of rest.

PART III

y daily life had changed all of a sudden!The approaching seven months seemed to me as big as an era! I was looking in the face of the biggest challenge of my life, and I knew that I would have to accept it all alone. I could not discuss it with any of my friends or relatives! Each day would bring along a new problem and I would look for ways to solve it. Like, I had instructed Uma to take complete rest. Now, Uma used to take care of all the household responsibilities, and in the event of her taking a break, someone was needed to perform her share of work. Who would take Prabhat to school? Who would serve him breakfast and other meals on time? So, Uma and I discussed these issues and we decided that we would not tell anyone for the next seven months that Prabhat was about to have a sister. We were well aware that our parents were critically ill, and if we told them anything, they would lose their sleep worrying about us and their health would suffer all the more. Uma said, "… but we will have to tell Prabhat about it." I replied,

"Leave it to me. I'll find a way to break the news to him."

Next morning, I took Prabhat to Brij Vihar temple. After performing *puja*, I said to him, "I need to tell you something, Prabhat. You know, God has granted our prayer. If all goes well, we will have Sugandh amidst us after 5-6 months. Your mother is not doing well, so do not disturb her anymore. If you need something, you should tell me. I will take you to school from tomorrow."

Prabhat listened to me, and turning his face towards God, said, "What is the point of sending her back now? By the time she grows up, I'll have gone abroad to finish my studies." I said angrily, "You should never speak to God in this manner. We should be grateful that He is sending her back."

I started getting up at 6 in the morning. I would get ready hastily, serve breakfast to Uma and then, drop Prabhat at school! Uma had not given up going to the hospital. In fact, it was not a big deal for her. Years ago, while carrying Prabhat, she had been at work until the day of her delivery.

Earlier, I would never lift a finger as far as household chores were concerned and now, I was performing duties at home and outside as well. I had no idea where I was getting so much strength from. It seemed to me that my daughter was making her journey back home. And she was returning from a place from where nobody had ever come back. I was full-heartedly prepared to do anything to welcome her.

All of a sudden, my mind wandered to the state of my own house. Forget about cleaning it, it had not been white-washed for years. I said to Uma, "Let's get the house cleaned and repaired immediately. We won't be able to do all this for the next two years. We will have to spend all our time in caring for the children until they are at least 1-2 years old." Uma replied, "How will you handle it all alone? It will only add to your burden." I tried explaining to her, "Trust me, it will not be difficult. Look, Sugandh's room upstairs is the biggest room and it's totally vacant. It was painted just six months ago. So, it won't need fresh painting. We will move all the household items into that room. Once the painting of the rest of the house is over, we will remove all the items." While I was mulling over getting these tasks done, Santu, who had been working in our house for the past 10 years found a job in a five star hotel. I could neither ask him to stay nor tell him how much he was needed in the house at the time.

I consoled myself thinking that it was again a part of the test that God was putting us through. I started redecorating the house. I had said very clearly to Kapil contractor, "You have only 20 days to finish the work because Prabhat's exams are around the corner and Madam is unwell. So, you will also have to take the responsibility of replacing the items. Madam has a leg-related problem, the doctor has advised her to take rest." The repair work in the house went on day and night. Santu reassured us that he would send his wife Savita to help us during the day until we had found a suitable replacement. It would ease our difficulties. It used to be very cold those days. Savita visited us for two days and then, she stopped coming. I was mad at Santu. Ten-twelve days passed. The work was about to get over. Then, one day, suddenly, Santu came running to me.

Before he could breathe a word, I burst out in anger, "Where on earth have you been? The work is about to get over and Savita appeared just for two days. I started this work counting on you people, and all of you have betrayed me." Santu listened and softly replied, "Sahab, Sugandh is present in the house." I said, "What nonsense are you talking?" He said, "Sir, Savita saw Sugandh in her dream this morning. She was picking up her stuff hurriedly off the floor and scolding Savita, 'You people have made a mess of my room! Clean it fast. God has told me that I will live in this house all my life.'" Santu's words made me shudder. Instantly, I raced towards Sugandh's room and found that it was chock-a-block with items. But my eyes were only looking for her in every nook and corner of the room. I immediately called up Kapil contractor. I told him, "Listen carefully. Get this room painted as well." He said, "But, Sir, you told me that it had already been painted some time ago." I said, "Yes, you are right, but the color is blue now, please paint it green. And change the floor tiles too. Change the bathroom tiles to something similar to what they are in Prabhat's room. Get a new AC fitted and redecorate the whole room." I thought, "Santu doesn't know anything. He has no inkling that Sugandh is present in Uma's womb!" All these incidents made me feel very close to God. I would keep praying to Him all my waking hours. We were so busy in these activities that we did not realize how quickly 6 months had passed. The doctor got the ultrasound test done when the seventh month of pregnancy started. Every doctor had been waiting eagerly for this test to be done. It was performed by the senior most doctor, Dr. Khurana himself. He conducted the test without any hurry. At 7 in the evening, he came out of his room and embraced me. He said, "I have been rewarded abundantly for giving my evening. Both children are in the pink of health and they are very active." I had two months left now. Uma had stopped going to the hospital. She had stopped stepping out of the house. The staff believed that Madam was unwell. But they couldn't even dream of the illness that Uma was suffering from.

Sarvar Khan, who was my assistant as well, alerted me. He said, "Sir, it is high time that we announce to the world that Madam is about to become a mother. Her delivery is due anytime now. If people are introduced to the children only after they are born, people might think that Doctor Sahab got these children through adoption. It would deprive the children of their due social recognition." I went straight to the temple and informed the priest about Uma's pregnancy. He told me about the *puja* that was meant for the seventh month of pregnancy. This ceremony required the presence of the sister and so, I invited my sister over to Delhi and got this *puja* performed following all rituals religiously. It did not take long for the rest of the extended family to know about it. Soon, my younger sister Karuna called up from Ahmedabad.

She said, "*Bhaiya*, you haven't yet sent me my share of sweets!" I said, "Sweets for what? We are so worried here and you are asking for sweets! One and half months are still left." Scolding her, I further said, "At the moment, just pray to God. You will get sweets when all turns out well." She said, "*Bhaiya*, could I ask you a question? Promise me, you won't mind!" I said, "No, go on." Karuna said, "You are a doctor. You would certainly know if the baby is a boy or a girl." I said, "Look, God has been with us till date. So, one of the children would be a girl for sure. Now, it doesn't matter to me if Sugandh brings along a brother or a sister with her. I would be glad if both children are girls. I will marry them off and will be free of my responsibilities very soon. We are doctors and we keep telling others all the time that it is a legal offence to determine the sex of the baby before birth. So, how can we break the law? I only wish for a healthy mother and healthy children." She said, "But *Bhaiya*, it will be the complete opposite of what you anticipate. Both children will be boys." I was stunned to hear her say that. She said, "I dreamt that both children were boys…and then, when Sugandh says, 'I will spend all my life in this house', it means that she will arrive as a boy. That is the truth." Her words made me sad but at the same time, I became fearful. I resumed visiting alone all the religious places during weekends. I visited Salasar Dham, Tirupati Balaji, Vaishno Devi, Ajmer Dargah and every other place where earlier I had expressed my anger,and there, I apologized vehemently in front of God.

"I was wrong! Please forgive me and let me have my family back." I offered two coconuts to every God and two *chadar* (shawls) at Ajmer Dargah. I wished for two healthy children and a healthy mother, who would bring them up nicely. I had full faith in my God. I could not attribute any single God for all the recent positive events. It seemed to me as if all gods had come together to help me out and in this *Kalyug* (Age of Kali), God had never made such close contact with humans as he was doing now.

My pilgrimage was over. The children could arrive anytime in the world. Uma appeared very weak and she was incapable of going out of the house. Before leaving for the hospital, it was necessary to purchase clothes for Uma and children and many other items ….and all these purchases are generally made by women themselves. It all seemed weird to me when I had to do these tasks. I went to the mother and child store and asked the manager to help me. I told him that my wife was ill and the doctor had advised her to stay at home. I bought milk bottles, diapers, baby soaps, and napkins. Then, it struck me, "What would children wear immediately after birth?" I went to Brij Vihar temple and collected the disposed old clothes worn by the idol. I got these clothes re-stitched for my soon to be born children.

I remembered God after collecting all these items. The doctor said, "Eight months are over. It is the right time. We shouldn't delay anymore. We will operate two days later with full preparation. Uma got admitted in the hospital. My doctor friends were ready. A large number of people had gathered in the hospital lobby waiting eagerly to hear the good news, and many more were praying in the temples or in their homes. The surgery started at 8 in the morning and exactly after 45 minutes, I received a call from Dr. Tiwari, who had been performing the surgery. Both children were doing fine. Within a few minutes, the news reached everyone. I took the elevator and carried the infants in incubator to the neo-natal ICU on the ninth floor. I was extremely happy to find the babies healthy. The nurse had made them wear the clothes I had got stitched for them.

It shocked me to the core to learn that both infants were boys. While I was preparing myself to accept this truth, I got a bigger shock when the nurse came running to me and said, "You are immediately needed in the operation theater." I went hurriedly and saw Dr. Gunjan waiting at the OT gate with a worried look. There were drops of sweat on her face. On seeing me, she said, "Uma is in a critical condition. She is bleeding continuously. We will have to perform a major surgery. Please go to the blood bank and arrange for 5-6 units of blood." Darkness descended over my eyes. It was really surprising that I did not faint. When I went downstairs, I found that the manager of the hospital himself was arranging for blood. He was saying, "Send blood immediately to OT! If there isn't any, I will get it from some other hospital or blood bank." My well-wishers had formed a queue and were donating blood. Reassured, I came upstairs to the doctors' room of the operation theatre and broke down in tears. My mobile was ringing continuously. People were making congratulatory calls but I was not in a state to thank them. I was dialing mobile numbers feverishly and pleading to my other doctor friends to reach OT and provide help. The doctors who came out of the OT had a dejected expression on their faces, and they were trying not to meet my eyes. Whoever I asked told me that she was very critical. I had only one thought in my mind now, 'No, it just can't be. This didn't occur to me even in my dream. I will jump off the hospital building and embrace death if I lose Uma today. How would I face Prabhat? He is at home waiting eagerly to meet his sister. He has been asking me repeatedly, 'Daddy, should I come to the hospital?' How can I ask him to come here? It is the same hospital from where I had apprehensively informed him of Sugandh's death, and today, I can't tell him, 'Son, in the greed of bringing back your sister, I have lost your mother too."

Finally, I was called in at 3 in the afternoon. Eight units of blood had already been given to Uma. She had regained consciousness. According to the doctors, she was more stable now but was not out of danger. She would have to be kept in the surgical ICU for the next two days. Her condition made me cry. I sat by her bedside for three hours. Quite a few blood samples had been taken from her. Now, I remembered Prabhat. I called him and got him to meet his mother first. Uma reassured him through gestures that she was doing fine. Then, it struck me that nobody had yet seen the newly-born infants upstairs on the ninth floor. I showed the two infants to Prabhat. His face lit up. I kept running up and down the whole night, rushing to the ninth floor for the infants and then, coming down to the second floor for Uma. I remained at Uma's bedside until morning. Dr. Chhabra's team arrived on round at 9 in the morning. Dr. Chhabra informed me that Uma was out of danger. I could not believe his words. I blurted out, "How is it possible?" she has been given eight units of blood. How can her kidney function test, hemoglobin, etc. reports be normal?" He smiled at me and said, "Brother, God is with you and now, the whole world is aware of it. Go take care of your family." Next day, Uma was shifted from ICU to the room. Now, the thought of the infants came to everyone's mind. The nurse brought the children to Uma for breastfeeding. I said to her, "How can a mother feed her children when she is in this condition?" The nurse replied, "I will surely try once. If there is no milk, the children will have to be fed with powder milk." Mother's milk is extremely important for the newborn. I came out of the room.

After a while, the nurse came out of the room looking very happy. I asked her, "Did the children get some milk?" She replied,"Both of them have had their fill." It is indeed very surprising in the context of medical science – a 46-year old woman giving birth to twins and feeding these infants the essential mother's milk. Uma's health was gradually improving. As per the doctors, she could go back home a week later. But I was apprehensive, 'How would we take care of the two infants and the mother?' Hence, I hired an ayah and a servant.

The infants were now two weeks old. Uma had gained enough strength to take care of them. It was decided that Uma and the children would stay in the room upstairs. It would allow Uma to take complete rest, and it will also keep children and her safe from infection. Eventually, the children had come back to Sugandh's room and settled in there. My sister, sister-in-law and Uma's parents, all set out to taking care of them.

Soon, the children turned a month old. Prabhat scoured the internet and chose two baby names. Keeping Sugandh in mind, we had to look for names that started with an 'S'. He named the boys "Samarth' and 'Shamak' respectively. When the news reached Parul and Shailja, they came running. I said, "Both of you had been making such a hue and cry with your 'Sugandh is coming, Sugandh is coming'. Now, tell me,where is Sugandh? These two children are boys." Parul looked intently for a moment at both the children, and immediately picked up Samarth and rested him lovingly on her shoulder. She said, "Uncle, this one indeed is my lost friend. We studied together since sixth grade.

She was the naughtiest girl in our class. We know her like the back of our hands. Have a look at his hair." I said, "Yes, I know. The nurse at the hospital also told me that it was the first time that she had seen a new-born with such long hair." Parul further said, "And Uncle. Please look at his eyebrows. They are very fine. If you compare them with that of Shamak, you will find that he has thicker hair. Also, look at his nails. She used to take great care of her nails. She has come back with the same kind of nails." Saying these words, Parul and Shailja took out black threads from their pockets and tying them around Samarth's wrist said, "May God protect you from evil eyes in this life."

I also realized that Samarth had a distinct body odor and it used to draw me towards him. While Samarth had a tranquil disposition, Shamak was more active and he used to cry more. As for what the astrologer had told us about the arriving baby that it would have a mole on its right shoulder, that mole was on Shamak's right foot big toe.Between these two children, which one was Sugandh? It was a big mystery to us. Uma was tormented by the fear that I would love Samarth more. I reassured her saying, "How is it possible? These two children are like my two eyes. How can I discriminate between them?"

Prabhat and I were happy. God had blessed me with much more than what I had prayed for. However, in the process of realizing my dream, I had become indebted to the whole world. I did not even know the names of those 12 people who had donated blood in the hospital for saving Uma's life. But I knew one thing. The first person to donate blood was my assistant Sarvar Khan.

When we left the hospital and reached home with the newly-born children, policeman Babu Khan Sahab's wife blocked our way and said, "We will make these children wear their first clothes. In order to bring these children into this world, we prayed so hard in the Mosque for two years that our knees are terribly sore." There were tears in her eyes and she added, "Every time I came to you for treatment, my heart bled to see the sad state you used to be in. On reaching home, I would tell Allah – Oh Allah! This man provides us with relief from our illnesses in a very short time, why are you making him live a sorrow-filled life?" The priests of the neighboring temples said, "We also used to pray day and night for you." A close relative told me, "You would have to come with me to Hardwar. I promised a *puja* on your behalf." Someone else was ready to take me to Varanasi. It increasingly appeared to me that I would never be able to repay their debts. I would have to take another birth to repay what I owed to all of them.

I was incapable of fulfilling the promises that I had made to Sugandh and Uma. Then, how could I fulfill the promises that I made to these innumerable people?

PART IV

Every day, I would stand before Sugandh's photo and implore to her, "My dear, please do come back to this world, I will always remain by your side. For you, I will forget everyone and everything. I will dedicate my whole life in keeping you happy. But I can't spend even a single moment without you. Having to live without you is such a torture!" On the other hand, Uma had been expressing her anxiety since the beginning. She would say, "You will leave these two newly born to my care and get busy with your patients. How would I bring them up on my own?" But I was very certain that the promise that I had made to God was far more important than the promises that I had made to both of them. In fact, I was supposed to fulfil my duty and serve my patients with more dedication. I put up a board outside my hospital which read that admission facility was open only for poor patients. I started providing medicines to poor patients and also lowered my fees.

God had trained the children very well before sending them to this world. Six months passed in the blink of an eye. Samarth had become very attached to me. He would sleep with none but me. Both children had adjusted themselves according to my daily schedule. They slept during the day and I would find them awake at 11 in the night.

An incident took place one day and I was stunned. Sugandh's friend Shailja had been visiting her sick mother and the lady was sitting in the clinic. Shailja had Samarth in her lap and was chatting with him. She was saying, "Samarth, look here! I have put yellow nail polish on my toe nails and red nail polish on my finger nails. You naughty girl, when would you begin with your pranks? This time you have arrived with full preparations, with all terms and conditions clearly defined by God himself. You wanted to be a boy, and that is the form you have taken in this life. You always used to keep your brother around, so now, you have brought along a brother with you. You wanted to have the same house and same parents. You were the drama queen of our class, and even in front of God, you have given a good performance." Samarth was intently listening to her. To me, all this was sounding very strange.

The ideas that the bestselling author Dr. Brian Weiss has touched upon in his book 'Many Lives Many Masters' were proving right in my life. I felt that Samarthwas my soul mate. I had begun to pay attention to his every little action. Like, when he slept, I would keep looking at his face again and again. Itseemed to me as if it was Sugandh, who was in deep slumber. However, I would spend same amount of time with Shamak. Both of them were equally important to me.

Gradually, nature herself sorted it out. Shamak started sleeping with Uma while Samarth couldn't sleep without me. A year passed with ease. Now, I was waiting eagerly for these two children to start speaking.Other family members including Uma were not ready to accept that Samarth was Sugandh. However, as far as I was concerned, both children were invaluable jewels that I had received as gifts from God. They had brought back happiness and prosperity in my life. They had brought back my long lost smile.

Shamak and Samarth were now two and half years old. Their walk, speech, running, everything was normal. Samarth fulfilled my expectations. He started addressing Prabhat, 16 years his senior, as 'Hey Prabhat', just the way Sugandh used to call him. Samarth and Shamak both used to address him as Prabhat. A few days later, he did something that once again surprised all of us. There was a bottle of Coca-Cola lying on the dining table and he began to call it Coca Lola. And then, he kept showing us with gestures how it should be consumed. Coca-Cola was Sugandh's most favorite drink. Or perhaps it would be more appropriate to say that it was the only drink she had ever liked. But she was forbidden from drinking Coca-Cola because of Asthma. So, she would drink Coca-Cola behind her mother's back. The two and a half year old Samarth used to spend most of his time in my company. In the morning, when I would be getting ready in my bedroom, he would come over and sit quietly on the bed. Earlier, Sugandh also would do the same on holidays. She would come and sit in my room. She also would carry the TV remote in her hand.

Since the day, Samarth had arrived in his mother's womb, I had developed an unshakeable faith in God. I was confirmed that this being who was about to arrive was certainly my Sugandh. I was not bothered at all about the form she had taken. And for this to happen, it was not necessary that Samarth or Shamak's every habit had to match with that of Sugandh's. God is capable of performing incredible things with supreme ease. It is blasphemous to cast a doubt on what he does. I was well aware of it. But other members of my family, my friends and my relatives did not believe me. They believed that I was delusional.

The two and a half year old Samarth had easily recognized the solitary City Center of the colony. Once, while standing outside the market, I asked him, "What do we get here?" and he replied, "They sell food inside". City Center used to be Sugandh's most favorite recreational spot. It was located on the way to her school. I used to ask her, "What is so special about City Center that Prabhat and you go there while returning from school and then, pay a visit in the evening as well." She would laugh and say, "Oh! There are so many things, like momos, mango shake, and much more."

Now, when the three year old Samarth sat in the car, he would always take the front seat. Uma and Shamak would sit in the backseat and I would be on the driving seat. Uma would repeatedly ask him to sit with them at the back but he would never listen to her. Finally, I would give in and adjust his seat belt. It seemed to me that by showing his wish to occupy the front seat every time, he was giving an expression to Sugandh's unspoken wish.

Earlier, Prabhat used to sit in the front seat. Uma and Sugandh would sit at the back. Sugandh would always express her displeasure to me about this arrangement. She used to say, "Prabhat is a boy and that's why you let him sit with you". I would reply, "No, He sits in the front because he is younger."

That's how, in this birth, God had granted Sugandh's small wishes also. She wanted to be a boy and sit in the front seat like Prabhat used to do. Oh, now, I had collected so many facts about rebirth. Their number was far greater than what I had read in all the stories dealing with rebirth.

I kept the promise I had made to God. I took Shamak and Samarth to every religious place and had them receive God's blessings in all the temples, mosques, and gurdwaras.

My OPD clinic had now acquired a totally different look. At present, I had lesser number of diabetes and blood pressure patients while there was a big crowd of grandmothers in the form of old women. These simple-minded women believed that I possessed a special kind of scientific technique using which I could help middle-aged women become mothers. They had begun to equate me with God and I, on the contrary, never wished to become one. It is a really difficult task to take God's form. At times, it becomes essential for God to take hard-hitting measures. The fun that one can derive from serving humanity in the capacity of an ordinary human being is totally absent when one is God. I would explain to people that human beings can make as much progress as they want but they can never conquer God. Only God can decide,in this world, who would arrive, when, where, and in which form.

There is no ultrasound machine available in this world that can tell who will be born as a boy and who will be born as a girl. No science can predict when and why you will leave this world. When a Hindu childless couple comes to me, before starting their treatment, I suggest them to visit Mata Vaishno Devi and Muslim Dargah of Ajmer. And, now I have so many questions whose answers may remain elusive for a number of centuries. For example, even after leaving the body, the soul speaks in the same tone as it did earlier. The difference between men and women is man-made. In God's world, they are just souls; they don't have any form. They are of two types, good and bad. Even bad souls are cleansed and their appearance is enhanced for sending them back to earth. There is no end to these ideas. Who knows, how many generations it would take to get an understanding of this mystery. Soul, God, the world, the other world, all this is impossible to fathom. But, we should always understand this, it is foolish to deny God's existence. Life cannot exist without God's blessing.

CONCLUSIVE THOUGHT

Grief can be so devastating and painful that it takes away all the joy from the life, making everyday functioning as unbearable burden. It literally takes your breath away. Loss of young child is an aberration from the natural order of things. The pain is immeasurable and unspeakable. Human beings can console you but cannot take away your grief.

It is only god who can lift the terrible burden of grief from your shoulders, so it is true that you should worship and remember god as much as you can during your bad time. Stress of grief can precipitate physical and mental illness. Keep hope. Continue to work as assigned to you by god. Time is a big healer. Dr. BRIAN WEISS, well known apiritual healer and best selling author of 'Many Lives, many Masters', also says Miracles Happens. Keep hope you may get your soul mate any time.